About the Author

A young lad who started on the rigs and travelled the world experiencing all that life could give. Now a man eager to share these thoughts.

The Travelling Rigger

Paul Lambert

The Travelling Rigger

Olympia Publishers
London

www.olympiapublishers.com
OLYMPIA PAPERBACK EDITION

A CIP catalogue record for this title is available from the British Library.

ISBN: 978-1-80074-419-6

First Published in 2022

Olympia Publishers
Tallis House
2 Tallis Street
London
EC4Y 0AB

Printed in Great Britain

Dedication

I dedicate this book to my wife Claire and our three lovely children, Lewis, Oliver and Ella.

Acknowledgements

Thank you to all my family for inspiration and guidance, without you all I could never experience what this world has to offer.

Thoughts!

My heart is yours
My soul you own,
You have me under your spell.
Anything I have is yours,
Let no one ever hurt you.
Beyond life I'll always be with you,
I'm proud to stand with you.
Distance can never part us,
You control every thought I have.
My wishes are your dreams,
Your smile is my reward,
Let nothing break our bond.

One year!

One year ago, with my eyes filled,
heart gleaming hand crushed and a room full of love.
We met for the first time, you never said anything,
just gazed,
at the voices you had heard for nine months before.
A princess arrived as a queen sat glowing,
A check and smile. It's a girl we see.
When I held you the first time I knew
my heart was lost for you,
Have taken all my love,
now two women control me for life,
A slave to your smile,
bound in a dream by your eyes!

Choppers calling!

"Attention all personnel, attention all personnel, chopper landing in thirty minutes all personnel, going off please come to the Heli lounge"
These are the words that we pray for, dream of and your heart starts to race.
Oh, if the land dwellers could only know this feeling.
Nothing we say can describe, can no land dweller know what this is,
this is our feeling and if truth be told, our drug that we keep taking!
Crew, lads together ready to take on anything and everything. "Barman, get the round in please", Oh the looks you get at 7am with a bottle of beer,
but the land dwellers just don't understand.
This is our time and our winning ticket, Lottery ticket winners we all, let's celebrate!
Baby I'm coming home!

From Another!

Five years ago, you stole my heart from another,
Each moment of thought you break me
Then make me whole again,
Each time I gaze upon your smile with eyes wide,
A doting heart is filled,
For such a small charm can demolish the greatest wall,
What I am, who I will become is forever at your side,
Without delay I will obey,
For you stole my heart from another!

To see you!

I lie here alone,
listening to music with your face burning my eyes,
The pain of not being with you hurts so bad.
Every clip of a film or shot of the TV makes me fill with
love,
Or sorrow that I'm not near you.
Oceans keep us apart, time lets the aching grow,
how I miss your smile
your eyes that melt the soul.
What is it all for, the long months apart, the days we miss?
Why the sacrifice is like the drug, we keep hating but keep
taking.
The feeling of not being with you kills,
but the feeling of seeing you grows and grows.
I love it but I hate it,
I want you yet I know it's for the best, A must to be apart.
What will this pain bring,
one day it'll all end,
then we'll watch, listen,
see everything that reminds us of the time we lost.
Never forget that love is stronger than the drug,
if you love someone so much you'll give them the world,
everything you are.
I miss you so much it hurts.
Can I ever show you how much I love you.
Tongues don't explain what the heart tries to say. One day
it will be clear that my soul is yours you see.

To see you again!

I close the door but it's never to lock you out!
I turn and walk away only to see you again!
I travel far and wide so that the future can be yours to enjoy!
The phone may not ring nor the iPad ping, but not as I don't want to speak!
Time rolls on but always remember …
I will see you again… it's never goodbye!

Miss your wing woman

Black eyed peas ringing out,
pint half full with one in the bank.
How you miss your wing woman.
Please let me share these times,
eye openers, happy faced people with the special one to me.
How do you explain what you see,
without annoying thee.
Please let me enrol on the course that stops you hurting.
Fountain in the centre of a street,
covered paradise for the party hard workers.
Three quarters of the pint gone,
fountain changing colour, how great is this place for thee.
Music running through every other,
Oh, special one why do you not see,
Would you please come see,
this place that shines so bright for me

What is happening

We witnessed something so horrific, has pushed our
society over the edge. now is the time to climb and do,
honestly don't know what it is,
Who should search for the answer. A lone soldier plunged
to lifelessness,
Daylight on the streets in a nation of peace. Who can
understand what one has witnessed, Yet the news came
out it was all true,
No dreams no nightmares just ugly truth. stab hack
scream, leave all like a stream.
True haunted cries but no just frozen statues in time, It
plays over and over,
scenarios how to stop what your eyes can see scum
stealing life in the daylight sun.
Gun, gun, let's think how could we get close. Horrific but
hope hearts don't bleed,
maybe jump in a car run that evil down. A hero gets close
why rush the attack, these butchers in broad daylight,
Waiting, waiting, waiting.
what they're trying to do use the day for Freddie's freak
display, Phones raised high people in horror to get their
post.
But why oh why didn't we cry scream rush the horror,
Now we know our haunted dreams walk the streets,
Families and monsters should never meet.

Sis

My big little sis,
we have shared our lives in fun and happiness,
the first real best friend who is always there night or day.
Happy times of you playing with your barbie whilst my action men fought with their tanks.
Following you like a lost puppy when you went to the park with your friends, "can I come" as I followed, with a response of "get lost".
To our secret antics of spending our garage sale money on sweets to you taking the heat or laughing together whilst we told of smashed Lladro.
We were happy all the time and lived through happy times.
We shared our joy and shared our sorrow, never shouting or fighting.
But when a shoe went swinging with the roar, "hit me then" but could never.
For you are my big little sis who I shall always protect.
From the lad at the bar,
To Mr happy on the street, all it takes is a flick of a heartbeat.
On your biggest fairy tale day,
I was able to stand and walk by your side.
With pride in my heart and a smile on my face.
You made me the proudest brother I could ever be.
I always know, no matter what time it may be,
A simple call is all you need.
We share our secrets and our troubles,
not one to solve but two can fix.

Some people think we're mad loopy,
but we're brother and sister, that all can see.
With love for each other.
Like you already know from years said,
I am your greatest birthday present.
Like twins we are not but a twin connection we have.
Your role in my life continues to play.
So let me just say for all to know, you are my sister and I love you so.
You are my big little sis, no present can ever replace thee,
but still remember I am the best present you ever had!

Journeys

Journeys push us to planes with no roads, Roads lead us
to avenues of unknown, Avenues come together to create
our web, Creation helps us find what we don't know,
Knowing happiness brings us all,
Happiness can't be rushed, can't be pushed, When your
journey opens the avenues,
You never knew excited then with it brings, Happiness!
Don't rush it will come!

WAITING FOR MY JET PLANE.

We sit we wait we loll around,
walking past strangers trying to look good feel cool but who do we kid,
what do they think,
Pushing shoving hurrying to be the first,
For what, cos the plane won't leave till the old lady gets wheeled down the gangway.
Sweaty feet, hairy arms from your travelling neighbour,
one touch comes the cringe,
Shrink in your seat so they don't touch you again.
Now comes the wobbling man, bump bump scrape and bang,
as he aims to tag everyone with his bag.
Up down they go till everyone's on, now buckle up away we go.
Grunt with a pump goes the hairy man, arms battling on the rest,
but no territory goes without the sly elbow or wobble,
how our temporary small space becomes a battle for the inch.
Quick let's do the good old sleep role and kick trick.
Now we're halfway through from night to day we go, how do we know,
cos some silly old fool likes to light up Broadway,
beams of light strike one head then the other,
no place for the dark or your eyes to hide.
But then comes the saviour stewardess,
Please consider the rest.

Riggers Delights

We are a brotherhood of no true calling,
We carry one bag,
Leaving all that is loved turning away time and again,
But one thing we fear that's not seeing our dearest,
We are ground in dirt and oil,
No shame to let your hands become tough,
Working day and night through all kinds of blight,
When that metal bird flies and that feeling becomes real,
Then you know there's no job,
that can create such true highs!
No mortal knows our true delights!

Who knows!

What drives one to be the way One is,
constant thoughts of wanting to prove who and what One
is, Willing and wanting to challenge,
fight for what is believed as right.
May it be lonely persons getting picked on, a Friday night
standing in someone's way, cos they are about to walk in
front,
push past a lady or some old fray, Mad thoughts
constantly rush through,
fuelling emotions from deep, do something anything,
feel like failing and need to make things right, who knows!
You're right!
Is it all down to childhood, a good happy childhood,
dwelled on the past always remembering being pushed,
not knowing how or when to fight,
Ask ya dad but never getting an explanation, just "go back
and make it right".
Scared of not knowing,
A battle fought oneself teaching that belief will conquer,
Bullies now friends,
who would have known,
the willingness to give everything and not give up.
Who knows!
What about every thought which flows, someone to come
and test thee,
push hurt the ones we love,
just to release what is trapped. Is it wrong we know,
terrible to think man what the feeling, standing eyes fixed

knowing,
this is your test, bruise me knock me down,
but watch out cos it will rise again, head racing.
No one knows, Who knows!

One Roughneck

Team, team, team, from an early age this is all you know.
Whether it's at school or on a Sunday with your mates at the footy.
So why should it be different at work?
It isn't and don't let people tell you it is.
We all want to be part of a team.
You create your team then everything else falls into place.
Helping each other and caring for each other.
Your team is sacred, it's our nature to be attracted to what you like,
same goes for people you work with as well.
So, the next time a miserable sod comes to the crew,
All moans cos it's clicky.
Explain the footy rule, it's just nature for people like you.
They know this but but can never admit.
Create your team and look after,
cos when you really need it, you'll know just how special it is.
To have your good footy team.

My promise to you!

As you pedal I will guide,
For every stride forever reach,
I promise you won't collide,
Just ride Just ride.

As you step out the door it may be blocked
but it will never be locked,
For I will always be ready,
Steady to guide you through,
Just knock Just knock.

Whoever wants to say,
May I take you away,
Hope they can say,
I'll stay I'll stay,
For my promise to you,
You're Never alone, Never alone.

On that day,
We will walk with gay,
As they all say, Hurray, hurray,
Your eyes will beam with each step of gleam,
My promise to you,
On that clear day, I will let thee stray.

My promise to you
Please let me stay
For I will still say,
I can guide each day.

Three amigos

When I think of three special diamonds,
When I leave every month it breaks my heart.
Sometimes thinking is it worth it,
what am I doing walking out that door?
But seeing their faces as I walk in brings pure joy,
my heart is swallowed in emotion of loving these three little amigos,
my greatest prize, my greatest achievement.
There's not a day I don't think about them,
as I do my heart swells and the throat tightens.
The pain cannot be explained.
Yet I know I have missed so much.
The biggest regret.
But then the days pass my amigos will know,
why we did what we did.
My life is for them to take,
I want nothing when I think or see them.
Just the feeling of a father, to them I can be.

Life Gone Day by Day

The start is release from the norm, As new life unfolds new areas explored,
We live for the challenge, We rejoice in the one,
As life gone day by day, 14-21-28 its all the same,
Fun to begin till the thought kicks in,
We seek each other as one, One is all for we all know the norm,

As life gone day by day,

Till time comes down we know no more, What was once rock tries to slip away,
We fret for the day a stranger who knows nah, Hold the rock so all is not lost,

As life gone day by day.

My girl

I will always be with you
Follow and care for you,
When your eyes water I will wipe them dry
If you're cold you will always know,
I will hold you till warm,
Never shall you be far enough for me to reach you,
For you will always see me though distance cloud me,
Even when you hate me, Angry with me,
I shall stand by you and wait till you look my way.
For I will not hurt you but always shy away,
For you are the most precious jewel one can hold
I can only stand and pray,
you will see what you mean to me one day!

Never forget

This is truly what our country is about!

Remember your past to carve your future!
Respect what has been to mould what is to come!
I see great things in all, let the poppy unite a great nation
to be proud of her history and not shameful of her
honours!
For she is our mother our body our soul!
She is in every one of us and let no person tear that away!
We respect we honour and we never forget!
We are united in our kingdom!

Blurred Vision

We walk around with our vision blurred by money!
Our life is controlled by pushing and shoving, striving to achieve more!
You step past without listening or understanding any reason!

Life is a team sport, you are not picked consciously even though you think you are!
Our subconscious speaks loudest all you have to do is listen!
Believe in yourself and those around you!

Missing You!

We write these things to you
puddles of words on a page,
sense lost in only our thought.
When they flow round one's head it's a dream come true,
a party, a movie it all makes sense,
But then it crashes to the paper and loses its being.
Oh look here's daft ideas swimming round one's head.
No one matters no praise is needed
just a look from you, a smile to show
it's all for you who could ever know.
These are the things we do for you.

Leave a mark

Smile and the light will shine on you! Say thank you and politeness will rain!
Make someone smile and you'll never be forgotten!
Make them laugh and your mark is sealed for them never to forget!

Leave your mark today!

Roughneck scratch!

Sharing is the way of life and never so more than when you're on the tin box.
Paired with your buddy sharing the room can be tough.
But there are some things you never can share.
In our beds watching the telly.
Coming from the other end of the room with a small creaking of a sound,
"Hey what you doing?" nothing comes the reply. "yeh whats the creak?"
Quick "shut it" is the answer. Now the mind is wondering as to what the itch is,
break the warm bed cover seal, just see what's happening.
Or should we just let the creak stay in our unknown.
"So what you up to?" as the covers rolled off.
"Check this out, look." We have a little friend.
The tin boxes worse fears,
Of unwanted little guests. Mind go racing as thoughts start to wonder,
"if I get these then you're explaining."
How do you say, hey baby you ok.
We had a funny old turn, but the doctors say ok, hey hey!
Oh, yeh she'll buy that I'll say.
So, after loads of abuse and a chopper ride to boot,
We burnt the bed sheets and flushed the itch,
But back as roommates,
You must always say,
Something can't share if you want to stay.

The cameo

The valuable lesson of showing but never doing.
Us roughnecks out on the rig floor in full view of the OIM & Toolpusher in the office as the V-door was open.
There we were scrubbing away giving it our all when the big chief walked our way.
"Right, you muppets, keep your heads down but nod every now and then, look what I'm pointing at and say sod all, A A, just nod."
As big chief kept pointing into thin air,
talking utter wobble but smiling wide,
after two minutes walked on by.
Just carried on doing what we had to do. Strange wonder running through.
Later when things eased off, we all asked big chief,
what's that all about,
"it's the cameo, they're watching in the window, and they see me giving you orders, bla, bla. We're the film stars putting on the show".
Big Chiefs leaving words were "now do one and leave me alone. If I need ya I'll call ya."
So that's the cameo.

ROUGHNECK OLYMPICS

A good event we use to always have on the rig floor as a roughneck was the test of the Olympics. The three of us had five events or tasks to perform and the fastest or the person who did the most was crowned champ. First, we had the timed choke valve closure. This was to close or open one of the choke manifold valves in the fastest time. Great for the little lads who at least had a chance of winning one event, ha, ha. Obviously, a watch was needed which sometimes came as a task in itself. Next, we had the eight-and-a-half-inch bit breaker press, great because it wasn't too heavy but just heavy enough to get the shoulders burning. This event was repetition, he who did the most won. One that I used to love, being a gym kid in my early twenties. Now this one used to come with its own controversy as what you count doesn't always add up to what your competitors count. Round three comes to a burner. Now this is my event, man or mouse. We have the burning tong jaw overhead press. Only one is needed or, if possible, for an instant first place, you could attempt two presses. But beware this is not for the twig arms as you can hurt yourself. We ain't talking about the small tong head either, it had to be the big head which had the three holes in. I've seen many a wannabe try this and never succeed. So here we are just the three of us and only me can lift the head, oh yeh one for the big fella. But I must admit my brothers in mud did try. So three events gone and here we are closing the games with just the last two. But as all great sporting events we saved the best till last. Strength here we come, first came the sub lift, nothing special but you had to pick up a sub of choice from the deck and just like a deadlift, you needed to lock your legs and hold it till the count of three. Now this was another feat in its self as the count only came from your fellow competitors or should I say mud brothers. We all know what conflict competition brings, so counting to three was a major feat. Lastly came the penultimate of events, the hammer curl to your nose. Now let me get this straight. This ain't easy so any attempt is cheered when a fourteen-pound hammer is coming towards your nose. It's all about the wrist, so the extra curriculum wrist exerts amongst us were very good at this. I must confess, I really struggled with this event, I think I needed more training in this particular sport. So guess who was good, yes the shy mud brother. Always early to bed.

So this concluded our roughneck games, which were always held every slow drilling day, which in the North Sea drilling into the reservoir gave us loads of time. So we became good at these events.

We had many more little warm-up events on the rig which catered for the operation we were doing. One good time killer, I mean team builder, was the eighty-five-ton shackle lift. Now everyone looks with amazement at this cos it's a big big shackle. But it's all about technique. Now I wasn't ready to tell the lads this though. The rules were simple, all you had to do was lift the shackle off the deck and place it on it hook which was about stomach height. Easy, so everyone thought. Even the big lads failed cos they had their backs arched and the weight was too much. So here comes Olympic organiser to show the Mud how to do it. With great pleasure I lifted it on the first attempt. But I must admit now, I use to do a lot of deadlifts in the gym so this was nothing. But as the rules go we never had to tell that, just do whatever event was put forward.

Oh, how I love a challenge. These were the great days of being a Roughneck working with the lads doing our Men's Men.

The roughneck musketeers!

The three of you, sweat brothers that never quit or let each other down. Time and time again you stand on the butchers table of mother earth, "pull" comes the cry. But you don't need the help as the three know each other's timing and strength. Like pistons in perfect unison, you all pull together. Together slips fly out releasing the mighty knife of the butcher. Down she goes. No calls are needed or looks, each man knows where to be what to do. One push of the foot and the knife is stopped, pop the elevators go with just the slightest movement, now it's the fourth's turn, we all glance up as he is the elevated one, top of the pack, leader of the mob. Crunch bang pop, the next knife is in and ready to go, brace wing and turn all together again, laughing loving the thrill. "Is that all you've got, pops?" we laugh and grin. The tally book distance with no mercy for fingers or the slow. In, spin, torque bend and bang we're off again. Oil doesn't call it, machine doesn't come close, it's more than that. This is spiritual, a bond that can never be broken. Looks can't enter, big mouths or wannabes can't handle. If you find it and you have it, no one needs to tell you, you just know. Let nothing break what is made or pint spilt spoil.

The challenge is set. It's your turn to test yourself and see the elevated one. Big breath as you climb the ladder, step by step, calls cry out that other men get offended, "curry stain" "limp biscuit is having a go" "this baby wipe can't even handle bog roll". Ha you love it, like words spoken to Juliet whilst in her tower. You're no frail mouse cos if you were you wouldn't be here, you passed the first day galley stare. Now you know it's all love that cries out. Laughter rains down. Round the corner you see the elevated one sitting chilling out rope harnesses, what's this some kinky foreplay. You wish. "I'll show you three" damn only three, now get on and have a go, lean out don't be an old Granny. If you miss I'll kick you off the board myself, ha comes the cry. Shit here's our yellow bus flying through the air, right ready rope in hand wrapped round my knife, everything starting to get tighter and tighter! Bang pop latch, shit I did it. Sit down chill then get ready for the next. Arms are pumping, hands are like G-clamps.

Right use the rope and swing out grab that front one, fuck I'm flying, superman style. jewels squeezing tight, oh what a thrill. No one can explain, we are the only ones who know, like the secret cults of the holy grail. This is our test, our thrill, our brotherhood. Cries fly up, faster here she comes, the yellow bus just doesn't stop. "Remember one thing," comes the great voice, "if she's empty fill her, if she's full empty her." Always one eye watching timing, knowing when to stand and throw your knife or wrap your rope and pull your knife back. Sweat starts to fall but the love is flowing and you can't stop, no drug gives the buzz. No matter where you look.

"Off" get back down you've had your fun, come back later okay. Damn no mercy from the elevated one, but he's one of us. A musketeer that knows the score, why he's the one who taught us all. Remember this is our time our space, twelve hours we rule the table and no one can come and sit without asking. Mud sweat everywhere brown chocolate glistening in the sun. Back down with the pack, no mercy or thanks but you know, you see what their eyes tell you. Smiles and laughter rain. "Come on snap snap" let's go we have knives to throw. Never stop never slow, never let your pack down. As this is our pack our team no blood is thicker or memory forgotten. Let no one break or divide no matter how hard they try.

And then it's gone, each ship sailing another course, but the memories are never forgotten, the tales never die. We just spread the word and create our own new packs, teach the bond cos that's the most precious thing.

No Coke and Mars bars can buy!

Printed in Great Britain
by Amazon

79810304R00031